MW01094236

Nothing is 100 Percent

My fight against brain cancer

Courtney Metrich

LifeRich
PUBLISHING
an imprint of The Reader's Digest Association, Inc.

LifeRich Publishing books may be ordered
through booksellers or by contacting:

LifeRich Publishing
1663 Liberty Drive
Bloomington, IN 47403
www.liferichpublishing.com
1 (888) 238-8637

Because of the dynamic nature of the Internet, any web addresses or
links contained in this book may have changed since publication and
may no longer be valid. The views expressed in this work are solely those
of the author and do not necessarily reflect the views of the publisher,
and the publisher hereby disclaims any responsibility for them.

Any people depicted in stock imagery provided by Thinkstock are
models, and such images are being used for illustrative purposes only.
Certain stock imagery © Thinkstock.

ISBN: 978-1-4897-0109-1 (sc)
ISBN: 978-1-4897-0110-7 (e)

Printed in the United States of America.

LifeRich Publishing rev. date: 1/31/2014

Foreword

While reading this I want you to know the two reasons I decided to write about my fight against brain cancer that began Memorial Day weekend in 1996. One reason is because I want my friends and family to get some sense of understanding of how much they helped me during my fight and how thankful I am to have them in my life. The second and most important reason I wrote about my story is for all the people who will be diagnosed with brain cancer and who will need something to read for support or hope. I want them to know that no matter what the prognosis is, there is always a chance of surviving. Always.

Now with that in mind, this is just me, talking to you. I didn't have an editor read this, and there may be a few errors, but that's not the point. The point is when I was diagnosed with an Astrocytoma Glioblastoma Grade Four brain cancer, I had no one to talk with who had been given the same diagnosis. And as anyone who has experienced cancer knows it is so very helpful, and gives so much hope when you know someone who has survived your same diagnosis.

There was nothing written about this brain cancer, nothing positive that is, and no survivors to connect with. So I want others to know I am a survivor and I want them to find hope in me. I did join a cancer support group at one time, but I was the most terminal case in the group, so that didn't help me much. Everyone was looking at me for tips and wanted to know what I did that helped me survive.

Though I did learn about the term "chemo brain" in my group, and that was so helpful. Finally, I knew why I couldn't remember what I did yesterday and that I wasn't the only one who was experiencing that. It was a side effect of chemotherapy. To make that connection with someone else was wonderful.

Regardless, I want other patients to have hope and know it is possible to survive for a long time. I want them to know there is someone out there who they can connect with, some-one who is willing to help and offer advice. So this is my story, and I hope it helps someone else win their fight against cancer.

The symptoms

I slowly woke up in the hospital bed with an extremely tight, white turban wrapped around my head from the brain surgery I had just had. My mom was sitting next to my bed. There was a knock at the door and in came my friend Annette with her mom Barb carrying a bunch of daisies to help bring my spirits up. Daisies were one of my favorite flowers at that time. They were so bright and happy, and that's what I needed to feel at that time. We were all waiting for the doctor to come in and give us the results of the surgery. Was the brain tumor they just removed malignant or benign? This was an answer we had been waiting to hear for an extremely long week.

It was May of 1996. I was twenty-one years old, attending college at the University of Wisconsin-Whitewater. I was at such a good point in my life. I was living in a big, old, brick house in Whitewater with eight other wonderful friends I had met during my college career. I was dating someone who I just loved, I thought he might be that special "one" and I was also getting ready for my student teaching. Finally, I was jumping into the real world of teaching. I was so very excited. Everything I had been working for seemed to be falling into place. It was a wonderful point in my life, so it seemed. But, I couldn't have been more wrong.

One morning I woke up with an incredible headache that had now lasted for two extremely long weeks. The college medical center was treating me for what they thought were migraine headaches. So I would wake up every morning feeling nauseous with a pounding headache and throw some drugs down my throat to stop the pain. The funny thing is, this seemed to help at first, but after a few days the pain continued to get worse. It got so bad I remember lying in bed trying to figure out how I could kill myself to stop the pain. I remember thinking maybe I could just step in front of a moving vehicle. That wouldn't take too much effort since I didn't have much to give. I eventually went back to the clinic and they gave me a shot of Demerol, which did wonders. For that night every bit of pain I had was completely gone. After having a headache and feeling like vomiting for two weeks this feeling was wonderful, but this time they told me if the pain came back to go to the hospital. And that is exactly what we did.

When I woke up the next morning I was in excruciating pain. This was the worst it had been. I tried to get myself out of bed for almost two hours. I knew my roommate, Amy was downstairs and could take me to the hospital, but I couldn't yell for her. I could barely talk because it hurt my head so much and I couldn't stand up because I felt like I was going to throw up all over the place. Finally I got myself to stand and slowly walked downstairs where my roommate was lying in bed. I asked her to take me to the hospital. She jumped up without a word and drove me to the Fort Atkinson Hospital about seven miles away. I thank God everyday for my good friends because they were there to help me over and over again throughout my fight, no questions asked, no hesitations. Once we got to the hospital, of course, the nurses were looking at me like I was some college kid just hung over from the night before, treating me as if I was no real emergency. "On a scale of one to ten how high would you rate your pain, ten being the worst?" The nurse asked me so many times I wanted to strangle her. I started answering with ten and ten and ten and finally said 100 as angrily as I could, which wasn't much at this point, I could hardly open my eyes from the pain let alone answer the same question over and over again. And Amy filled out all of my medical forms. So they gave me some more Demerol and threw me into the CAT scan machine and that's when we found out the horrible news.

Discovery

I was lying on the stretcher in the emergency room when the doctor woke me up. He was kneeling down on my left side to be face to face with me, and Amy was standing on the right side of me. The doctor said, "Okay Courtney, you're going to need your friends and family right now to help and support you. You have a brain tumor." At this point I was so drugged up that what he said really didn't register with me. I said, "Okay," in kind of a soft, weak voice, looked over at Amy and asked, "Why are you crying?" I'm not sure what her answer was, I don't remember much after that.

The next thing I do remember is, I woke up in my own bed back at the house from my roommates shaking me and saying, "Wake up Courtney, you have to take this medicine. We crushed these pills for you and made a shake so you can drink them through this." At that point I wasn't able to swallow pills. I always got the liquid form of medication when I was sick. My roommates continued to say, "We called your parents, and they're on their way down." My parents were living four hours north of me at that time in Lake Tomahawk, WI.

I slowly sat up and started to look around my room feeling a little unsure of what was happening. I mean, I knew what was happening. I was just still processing all of it. I turned my head to the left to find a fluffy new teddy bear next to me with a long skinny vase filled with yellow tulips the girls had picked from around our house. A small piece of masking tape was wrapped around the vase that had been written on with black marker. "We love you, The Zodiac," it said. The Zodiac was the funky name we picked for our house, so in other words, love, all of the girls. This was the beginning of the new life I would find myself living.

That night my mom called her best friend and found out going straight up to Mayo Clinic would be our best choice. So that's what we did. The next morning my parents and I had to leave. We were going to Mayo Clinic to get the best surgeon, no messing around. My mom's best friend happens to be a doctor and told her that Richard Marsh was the best and we should ask for him. I will never forget that day. As I walked down the steps of our house that morning with my head finally clear I said silently, "God, I need you now."

I had been living with my friends in college for four years by that time. We had built quite a bond between us all. We weren't just friends anymore. We were a second family to each other. I didn't want to go with just my parents to Mayo Clinic. I wanted my friends to come with me. Why couldn't they come too? We were each other's support now. I wanted them to come too. I needed them there with me. Well, I had to go and of course they couldn't stop their lives and come with me. Barb was waiting downstairs and told

t worry, my step dad has had brain tu-
:y'll take it right out and you'll be fine."
Hearing that made me feel a little better, but I
still didn't want to go. Amy gave me her brown
cereal bowl and green spoon so I could crush
my pills and mix them with some applesauce to
make swallowing the pills easier. That bowl and
spoon were better than nothing. It was a little
piece of the girls I could keep with me on my
scary journey.

The waiting

When we arrived at Mayo Clinic we found out we had to stay for almost a week before surgery. The first doctor asked us how we found out about Dr. Richard Marsh. He didn't know if was available, but said he would try to find him for us. He did end up finding him and we were able to meet with him. Dr. Marsh told us we wouldn't know anything about the tumor until the surgery was complete, meaning he couldn't tell us whether it was benign or malignant by just looking at the scan. However, I had a feeling he did know what the outcome was going to be. It was the way he spoke in one of his sentences, and maybe the way he looked at me. I got that sense that he was feeling bad for me already. He was a very nice man and told everything like it was. I asked what exactly happens during a brain surgery and he explained it in very simple terms. "We shave your head, use a little saw on your skull and then crack it open, take out the tumor, put your skull back together and sew you up." He made it sound so easy.

So for the next week we stayed in a hotel while we were waiting for the surgery to happen. Every morning we took the shuttle from the hotel to Mayo Clinic. We would board the shuttle with all of the other sick people from all over the world coming to Mayo Clinic for help. We would go from the hotel to Mayo, from Mayo to the hotel. I couldn't believe I was one of those people now. Our day consisted of spending hours at the hospital for tests, blood work, and doctor talk. My dad was always carrying around a small blue cooler filled with Amy's bowl and spoon along with my applesauce and medication. Sitting in waiting rooms looking at all the sick people and thinking, "Oh, my, gosh, I can't believe I'm here" became a daily routine. Then we would shuttle back to the hotel where my mother had a stockpile of lemon-lime Mister Mistys from Dairy Queen in the hotel freezer for me. That was the only thing that helped reduce my nausea caused from the steroid I was taking to reduce the swelling in my brain.

My dad had to eventually leave Minnesota for work which left my mom and I together for a while just sitting around waiting for surgery. What did we do? Well, I talked on the phone with my roommates every night. One of them would call and we'd do group hugs over the phone and talk about how for some reason all I wanted to do was garden. I still don't know why I was feeling that way. Maybe it was the simplicity and quietness of being in a garden surrounded by beautiful flowers that gave some sort of peace in the chaos that was going on in my life. We also talked about school and what was going on there because I wanted to maintain some type of normalcy. I recall one of my roommates saying, "Oh, you'll be fine. It has to be fine. Don't worry." It was at that point that I realized how different our lives had become in just a matter of days. I was living this real thing that was really happening and she was one of those people I used to be, thinking something like that would never happen to me. Aren't we all that way? Thinking, "Oh, you'll be fine, you have to." But this was my life now. This real thing was happening to me and no, we don't know that I'll be fine. It doesn't have to be nothing just because we can't believe this is happening. It is something, and it's definitely happening.

We were still stuck in this hotel room and I was still nauscious all day long so other than talking with my roommates to help me feel better, my mom and I talked about almost every funny story from college I could think of. I wanted to feel good and feeling good to me meant laughing. This meant any goofy things my roommates and I did during college, and any, forbidden-to-tell, stories came out of me and went straight to my mother. And no, she probably didn't want to hear some of those stories, but those stories were the reason we laughed the entire time we were lying on those hotel beds.

Finally, the day came for surgery. I remember my dad saying, "Everything's going to be fine, I know that because I saw a rainbow while I was driving back and you used to draw rainbows all the time when you were a little girl." That thought made me feel a little better. I think we were all feeling pretty good about the surgery. So back onto the shuttle heading for the clinic is where we went. Of course I was extremely nauseous because you can't eat or drink anything before surgery for fear of vomiting from the anesthesia. When we arrived at the clinic I had to lye on a stretcher while a nurse prepped me for surgery. The nurse asked me to stick out my tongue and then she gave me this really weird look, like she was kind of scared and didn't know what was happening. That completely freaked me out and I asked, "What?" She responded in an unsure voice, "Your tongue is green." Oh, it was just my tongue. What a relief. Remember I had been eating Mister Mistys from Dairy Queen all week. Those are green. We shared a little laugh after I explained that to her. Next, I went in to see the anesthesiologist. He explained he would be giving me a shot and would like me to start counting at one and that I would eventually fall asleep. I remember saying "One, two," and I was out.

I don't remember a thing after that until the nurse started asking me to wiggle my feet and move my arms so she could see if there were any side effects from the surgery. I was now in the recovery room with a turban wrapped around my head and a tube coming out of head draining something into a clear plastic container. I don't remember much else about being in there. Eventually I was moved into a hospital room with my mother, Annette who had just brought in flowers, and her mom. We were all waiting for the results of the surgery. If you've ever worked with doctors or hospitals you realize how extremely long this process can take. The waiting is the worst.

Finally, the doctor walked in. Annette and her mom walked out. Was the tumor malignant or benign? I knew what the answer to that question was the minute the doctor walked in the room. I had never in my life seen a look on someone's face like the look that was on that man's face. Nor do I ever want to see a look like that again. I knew that what he was about to tell me was bad, so bad that I could feel his dread and sorrow before he said a word. He grabbed a chair and pulled it up to my bedside. I slowly rolled over onto my left side to see him. My mother sat close by. What he was about to say to us would permanently change the way I lived my life.

Diagnosis

You have cancer, cancer! cancer! is how it echoed in my mind. "Astrocytoma, Glioblastoma, Grade Four. We removed the tumor from your head, but it will come back within the year and you will die," is exactly what he said. "Well, what are the chances?" I asked. "100 percent," was his reply. Let me summarize that. I was twenty-one years old, in my last year of college and I was just told I was going to die within the year. Any chance I could pull through this? Nope. The doctor said with 100 percent certainty I was going to die within the year. In reality 95% of people once diagnosed died within 6 to 9 months of diagnosis. I think I stared at him for thirty seconds trying to understand what he just said to me. My first clear thought was, "I'm not going to graduate college!" I know that sounds like a silly thought to have when your life would soon be ending, but then again, I don't know what a normal thought would be when a person is told they're going to die.

Graduating college meant so much to me because my dad once told me I would be the first Metrich to graduate from college. This meant a great deal to me as a young girl wanting to make her father proud, and I wanted to accomplish that goal.

After that passing thought I turned to my mother to cry. The doctor left shortly after that and a few minutes later the chaplain came in. Oh. My. Gosh! was my thought. The chaplain was there to talk with us because I was going to die! Was this real? How could I be in this situation? What was happening? This isn't right. Somebody, please wake me up! The chaplain sat down and asked us if we needed anything or wanted him to say any special prayers. My mom put her hand on my head as she started to cry and said, "Just for Jesus to touch her head with his hands and heal her."

I still couldn't believe this was happening. It all seemed to be like something I would watch in a movie. It was almost unbelievable. A little while later a different nurse came into the room to describe the type of tumor I had in more detail. She said generally, and what I mean by generally is 95 percent of the time a patient will die within six months of diagnosis. I asked if anyone had ever lived longer than six months. She reluctantly replied with, "Well yes, ten years. The longest is ten years. It has been done, but it's not likely." That was it! That's what I needed! It's been done! Not everyone has died in six months! It's been conquered! I can do it too! And that, is what we call hope. And it was at that moment that I started living on it.

The recovery

I finally returned from the hospital to my parent's house to recover from surgery. I will never forget that day. My mom helped me into the house and I saw a big welcome sign and the room was filled with flowers. When I say filled, I mean filled. The entire room was filled with flowers. It looked like we lived in a floral shop. I was shocked! I assumed I would have some flowers, but oh my goodness, it was amazing! I never realized how many people cared about me. And that wasn't the end of it. Everyday while I was recovering the florist van would come down the driveway with another delivery. We would look at each other and laugh because it was so amazing. And that is what I call my support. My love and my support.

I was so happy to be out of the hospital. Anyone who has ever had any type of surgery understands that the hospital is no place to rest. The food is horrible and just when I would fall asleep, which wasn't easy with all of the needles that were connected to me and the turban wrapped around my head, another nurse would come in to give me medicine or take my temperature. So being home with my parents was wonderful, although I found myself in a unique situation. I was twenty-one years old, fully capable of taking care of myself, but I needed my mom to wash my hair and help me take a bath. Part of the recovery process was gaining my balance and strength back to be able to do those things on my own.

While I was recovering my wonderful friends came to visit and I had expressed my fear about the guy I was dating. I thought for sure he would leave whatever it was we started because of this diagnosis. They reassured me of his support, even suggested he would go so far as to shave his head to make me feel better. Well, the problem with cancer is it interrupts everything in your life. Whatever you may be involved in will need to stop instantly, just for the time being so what needs to be taken care of is properly taken care of. Needless to say, that guy was out faster than I could say his name. I don't care to think of him anymore, it just brings negativity into my life.

But the girls came with tons of other good information. They did plenty of research before coming to visit me and found out that I wasn't going to lose my hair during chemotherapy. I was so excited to hear that. Even though losing my hair was the last thing I should have been worried about, it was a big thing. Being sick was bad enough, but being sick and losing my hair made it worse. After discussing all of the facts about this illness, came the big question from my friends. "We heard you only had a year to live, is that true?" "Oh no, no," I replied. And I still don't know why I couldn't tell them the truth. I felt like I would be letting them down if I told them I was going to die. Then, of course, after much research on the cancer that fact did come out on its own.

Now we had to discuss room arrangements in the house for next fall. I was going back to school even though all of this was going on. I was not going to quit. I was going to push through and get it done. I did have to postpone my preschool student teaching for the following semester. But see my radiation doctor told me I would be so exhausted by the end of the seven weeks I would almost need to be carried out of the hospital, so my friends put me in the room on the first floor of the house when it was my turn to be upstairs. They thought they were doing a good thing, but I explained to them, no. We are not going to believe what the doctor says are the typical side effects. I'm going to take the treatments and believe that I will be just fine, and able to walk on my own. I was going to take the room upstairs. So I took the room upstairs. I had read previously that patients should not ask what the side effects of certain treatments were, because just knowing the side effects causes some people to get them due to the suggestion of thought.

Radiation
Treatments

After recovering we had to focus. What next? The tumor was out and there were still little microscopic veins of cancer in my brain. I wanted it out! I felt dirty, like there was something dirty inside of me. I wanted it taken out as soon as possible. Our first step was finding an excellent neurologist. Dr. Marsh had suggested Dr. Nicholas Vick out of the Kellogg Cancer Center in Evanston, Illinois. We chose Dr. Vick because Mayo Clinic was very comfortable with him and we asked him how he felt about alternative cures and other things available that might help me. He answered, "You do what you have to do, I'll do what I have to do, and together we'll fight this. That was exactly what we were looking for.

In the midst of all this recovery everyone was doing research on this type of brain tumor, my friends, immediate family, aunts, uncles, and cousins. In doing so they found many different alternative therapies in fighting cancer that we were going to try and wanted to make sure my doctor was on board with that.

The next step was the plan of action. Dr. Vick said I would need seven weeks of radiation treatments and if the cancer came back after that we would move on to chemotherapy. I had to move in with my grandparents in Illinois because the hospital we were going through was in Illinois. Why didn't we use a hospital that was closer to my immediate family? Because we were using nothing, but the best, and that meant living in Illinois for a while. The doctor explained to me that they would be giving me the highest dose of radiation possible and that I would lose my hair and probably wouldn't be able to walk out of treatments towards the end because I would be so exhausted. I'll never forget that first day.

I had to lie down on a cold metal table with four radiologists standing up surrounding my head. Then I saw the big piece of plastic looking saran wrap type thing they were going to place over my face. What?! Weren't we always told never to put that kind of thing over our heads in fear of suffocation? And now here come my radiologists with just that. Oh, rest assured though, there was a tiny hole for my nose to allow for some breathing. What was this for? They needed to make a mold of my head so they could lock me into the same position everyday on the table and line me up to this red beam that went to this tiny, tiny, tattoo they put on my head in order to get the radiation to the exact same spot everyday. Wow, that whole day was pretty scary.

After that, every radiation treatment was a piece of cake. My dad's friend would pick me up every morning; we would drive an hour to the hospital. I would go in and lye down on the table and they would line my tattoo up with the red beam and radiate me for all of two minutes; I guess is how I would say it. We would then turn around and drive an hour back and do the same

next day for the next seven weeks. My
and I used to joke about me going in and
saying, "Beam me up Scotty." We found humor
in everything, which was weird because I never
thought I could deal with something like this, but
we laughed constantly. I was just given six months
to live and we laughed all of the time. Why? Because laughter is the best medicine. I know that
to be true. Laughter heals people.

Don't misunderstand me though, there were
many times I would cry in fear of what was happening. Not when I was around my family, I kept
these tears for the night so no one could hear me.
I didn't want my family to worry more about me
than they already were. It was when I was around
my friends that I could let those tears out. It's different with friends. I knew they wouldn't worry
like my family. And the wonderful friends that I
had would just listen and listen while also trying
to offer support. I remember Amy said to me one
day, "Court, I don't know what to say anymore."
I replied with, "You don't have to say anything.

Just sitting and listening to me helps so much." I will never forget that moment because it reminds me of how much of a role my friends have played in my recovery. I had such a good support system with my friends and family to lift me up when I was down, I can understand how people might not do so well without the support of others.

Alternative Treatments

While staying with my grandparents my Aunt Kris flew in from New York. She had been researching alternative therapies for terminal illnesses and my mom and I were reading as many books and articles that we could get our hands on about cancer. The causes, the different treatments and anything else we could find. My aunt had found several stories of people miraculously healing themselves from terminal illnesses by continuously laughing. There is book titled, Anatomy of an Illness, written by Norman Cousins that discusses this exact idea. Well, we were already on track with that alternative therapy since we were laughing all of the time. My younger cousins Ashley and Megan were a big help with that, we laughed about the goofiest things all of the time. It was reassuring to me to find out that people had actually cured themselves with laughter. That gave me a little more hope. First, that someone survived ten years and now laughter. Those were two good things lifting my spirits up.

My aunt had also introduced me to Dr. Bernie Siegel's books, Peace Love and Healing, and Love Medicine and Miracles. I listened to the audio-tapes instead of reading the books everyday on the way to radiation treatments. Just listening to his voice was soothing in itself. He talked about why people become ill and different ways to heal your own body. Listening to him was when I learned about the technique of visualization. He discussed different ways to visualize the cancer away. While lying in bed with my eyes closed and visualizing PAC-Men eating away the cancer, or maybe a bulldozer plowing the cancer away and many other examples. I think I started with the PAC-Men, but then I changed to using a pencil eraser to erase the cancer out of my brain. This technique is something I still use every night before I fall asleep. I learned a lot about the power of the mind from him and this is when I realized one of the courses of action I would take to cure myself from this cancer. I would think it away.

Now remember my mom and I had been reading several books about cancer and alternative therapies. What we seemed to have found, to break it into bottom line, the simplest of terms, is that cancer is caused from a low immune system. Now that all made sense to me because I was always sick. Growing up I always had strep throat and anything else I could pick up. Put me around someone with the flu and it was a guarantee I would get it. So realizing, bottom line is low immune system made perfect sense. So what did we have to do to fix it then? After researching we found out how many vitamins and what kind of vitamins a person needed who was going through radiation treatments and who was fighting cancer. What it came down to was me carrying a small box around filled with Shaklee vitamins. I took Shaklee vitamins because they were completely organic which meant I knew exactly what I was putting into my body when I took the pills, and that it was exactly what I needed. The box was divided into sections kind of like a box filled with different fishing lures. Each section was labeled with a sticker naming the kind of vitamin and amount I needed to take each day. I was taking a total of thirty vitamins a day including, B complex, vitamin A, vitamin C, vitamin E, garlic, beta carotene and many others. This seems like a lot, and it was a lot, but I was fighting cancer which meant my immune system was down and needed to get back up there to fight. And remember, I still couldn't swallow pills at this time so I used a pill crusher every time I had to take the vitamins, mixed them up with some applesauce and then swallowed them. Fun, fun, fun, I write, sarcastically.

In addition to those thirty vitamins divided up between my three meals I was also taking a few teaspoons of shark cartilage three times a day along with a glass of pure carrot juice everyday. Why was I taking shark cartilage? Because sharks don't get cancer and there were several books written about how taking shark cartilage cures cancer. We even talked with the people selling the cartilage to ask if it worked on brain cancer and they reassured us it did work. See the thing with brain cancer is there is a brain barrier that only allows certain things to pass through to the brain which is why it's so hard to cure. Doctor's hadn't found a drug that could pass through the barrier to penetrate the cancer site. So when we talked with the people selling the shark cartilage and they said it worked with brain cancer we were on board.

Now I know some people reading this, are thinking, fools, we were scammed. But let's think about that, when you are given six months to live, you try everything, there's no time to be skeptical, no time to question, no time to think, you just do it. And oh, my, gosh that shark cartilage was absolutely disgusting, but in my mind I had no choice. Do it or die. The carrot juice we found out about through my cousin Paul. He said he had heard about people being miraculously cured from terminal illnesses by drinking carrot juice everyday. My cousin Paul bought me a juicer and we made pure carrot juice everyday. One bag of carrots made one glass of carrot juice. So I was drinking one bag of carrots a day. I didn't particularly like the carrot juice either. I guess you could say it was kind of a good thing I had been in college the last few years because I could slam that carrot juice like I was at a house party.

Side effects
of Radiation

For the first few weeks of treatments I stayed with my grandparents and a couple friends came to visit while I was there. Once again I need to point out how supportive my friends are and how much they have helped me fight this disease. After a few weeks I moved in with my cousin Heather and her husband Kevin just for a change of scenery. Heather thought it might be nice for me to switch places for a bit. After some thinking I agreed.

One of the first few nights I was there my friend Rachel came to visit and we all ordered Chinese for dinner. After dinner we were opening our fortune cookies. Now I'm not superstitious, but I do believe in God. Without a doubt, I know there is a God. I have had many, many, experiences in my life with God to think otherwise. So I was opening my fortune cookie and it said, you have an iron construction. I think I yelled, "Oh, my, gosh! Did you hear that? I have an iron construction! That's a sign from God! I'm strong enough to fight this. I'm going to be okay!" Anyone else in that room could have gotten that cookie, but they didn't. At that moment I knew I was going to be okay. I can't explain to you how excited I was. I felt like God was really talking to me. But wait. That's not all. My next cookie read, time is the wisest healer. What? Another sign! Time! In time I will be okay!

Wow. What a night. I will never forget that night. I know some people will think that's crazy that I believe that and just coincidence and God doesn't talk to us through fortune cookies, or what a fool I am to believe such a thing. But you see, that's how I came to be a survivor. That belief is what makes me strong. Believe it or not is up to you, I do. And that trust in God is why I am here today. During that summer I read the Bible, almost every free minute I had and came to the verse that said, the impossible is possible with God. When I read that statement I got so excited and thought, oh, my, gosh! I can survive! The impossible, which is what I had, was possible with God!

Well, I can't say every night at Heather's was as exciting as that one, but it was a very good idea to have moved me in because it was in the next few weeks that my hair started falling out. This was one of the scariest times for me during my eleven years of fighting cancer. I will never forget the first moment. I was in the shower and I noticed big chunks of hair falling to the bottom of the shower. I was completely freaked out and started yelling for Heather, my hands were shaking. "My hair is falling out!" Now Heather's a nurse so she ran in and was able to calm me down completely with her slow, calm voice. "Okay, the doctors said this would happen, it's okay, just try to relax." Thank God I was at her house because I needed a nurse at that time. During the next few weeks the rest of my hair continued to fall out on both sides of my head. I was lucky though, it was only on the sides of my head where the hair was falling out. With brain cancer, the hair falls out because of the radiation treatments, not the chemotherapy. So I had one perfectly round bald circle on both sides of my head. However, I'm blessed with extremely thick hair so I could pull the hair on the top of my head down to cover the sides. I wasn't very comfortable with that though and my bangs were shaved off so for the majority of the time I wore my blue bandana.

Uncomfortable
Moments

During that stay with my grandparents I was wearing my blue bandana around my head and at that point half of my head was shaved like a soldier's hair is shaved off. And along with that half of my bangs were shaved off and I had a horseshoe-shaped scar that was all stitched up on the right side of my head. If you saw me without the bandana you might have thought I was right out of a horror film. Well, we went to eat lunch one afternoon at Ed De Bevics downtown Chicago. While we were waiting in line in the restaurant to be seated a waiter comes by and grabs my bandana off my head and says, "Oh, your hair can't be that bad." Oh my goodness, if you could have seen the look on that man's face. Remember, I look like I came straight out of a horror film. I've got stitches, only one side of my head is shaved, there's dried blood. I think his face went white. While my relatives were reprimanding him and explaining I just had brain surgery, I was letting him know, "It's okay, it's okay, don't worry." I felt so bad for the guy he looked like he was going to cry. I guarantee he never pulls another bandana off someone's head. It's all pretty funny when I think back now.

Oh, and that wasn't my only uncomfortable moment. I eventually started to be more comfortable with leaving my hair pulled down over the sides and not wearing a bandana, which was still a pretty rare occasion, but I did go out and about like that every so often. One day my mom and I stopped at the gas station to get some gas. I ran inside to pay the attendant, remember half of my bangs are shaved off, and she says, "Don't you think you cut your bangs a little too short?" What?! Did you seriously just say that, is what I was thinking at the time. I finally had the courage to go out without the bandana on my head and that is what someone says to me! And since when do we make rude comments about other people's haircuts in the first place? Aren't we supposed to keep any rude thoughts we have to ourselves? Maybe that's just me, but oh, my, gosh, I couldn't believe it. My response to that rude woman was a calm and cool, "Nooo, I just had brain surgery." Now embarrassed by her own comment she said, "Oh, well everything is okay though?" And my excited response because I could see she felt like a complete idiot was, "No, it was cancer and I'm going through radiation treatments right now. Thanks, and have a good day." Wow, what a good comeback! I felt fantastic after what first began with me feeling extremely uncomfortable. People are weird. I've come to learn this through my experiences with life.

Moving on
With Life

At the time I was diagnosed it was the end of my fourth year in college in Whitewater, Wisconsin. How was I going to manage this was the big question. Do I continue with college? I was supposed to start my student teaching. How would that work out? I was living with eight other roommates, are they going to want a sick person there hanging out all the time? Should I just take off and live with my parents for a while? I had two choices, go back to college and fight as if nothing was wrong or drop out and succumb to the prognosis I was given.

Hell no! I was going back to college. My choice was to live. I was going back to college and would continue on with the course of my life as if this was just something I needed to deal with and would eventually be over. So I went on to speak with my professor who postponed my

41

student teaching until I was stronger and I took some low-key courses while going through my next set of treatments, which was chemotherapy. TNP 470 was the name of that drug.

Now that my radiation was over I had to take chemotherapy because the radiation didn't get rid of the cancer, but now I was in Whitewater which put me an hour and a half away from the hospital I needed to go to for treatments three times a week. How did I handle that? Well, once again, my wonderful friends/roommates jump in to offer their help and support. Each day I went to chemotherapy one of them would drive there with me and stay with me for the hour-long treatment and then we would drive back to school. How incredibly boring for them that must have been, but they did it without hesitation. Oh, but we wouldn't just sit there. I remember one day Rachel held onto my medicine pole while I sat on the little chair with wheels and we zoomed across the room, from one end to the other. She held onto the pole and would run on the side so the needle wouldn't rip out of my arm. That still makes me laugh today. It's all about a good attitude. If I wanted to heal myself I needed to keep my spirits high. We were goofy and laughed as much as we could, even during chemotherapy.

October eventually came which meant I needed another MRI scan to see if the cancer was gone or if it had come back again. A few of my friends came with me to the doctor's appointment with me for support. Anyone who has fought cancer understands the amount of stress that's involved in waiting for the scan results. My stomach was turning, my hands were shaking, and I couldn't stop looking down the hallway for my nurse to call us in. It's a horrible morning before the results of a scan. We were finally called in to see Dr. Vick and that's when we heard the bad news. The cancer is back again. Okay, what do I do next? There's something inside of me that's not supposed to be there. I want it out! The option was gamma knife surgery. Fine, let's do it quick.

October 24 was the date we set for the gamma knife surgery.

For those of you who have been spared the cancer fight let me explain that the gamma knife is something I couldn't believe was allowed in to-day's day and age. I sat in a chair surrounded by doctors as they numbed my skull in four different places, two in the front, two in the back, and then they placed screws into my skull so they could later attach a five-pound piece of metal or "halo" as they called it onto the screws. This was done so they could lock me onto the radiation machine to precisely radiate my skull in the exact spot that needed to be radiated. Oh, my, goodness! While the screws were being placed into my head I asked the doctor, "Are you sure you're doing this right." I just couldn't believe something like that was allowed today. It was like something out of a science fiction movie. But that wasn't even all of it. I had to wear the five-pound piece of metal all day long, from nine to five, before they could lock me up to the machine. Wow. Talk about a day. As the doctors and I walked out of the room into the waiting area one of the doctors said to my mom, "You've got a tough one here." She replied with, "She grew up with three brothers, she had no choice." My friend Barb was also there with me. Thank goodness because, eventually, not being able to move my head for hours started to hurt. My mom and Barb both helped by massaging the back of my neck a little to relieve the soreness. Finally, I was locked into the radiation or gamma knife machine which I think took all of five minutes. The doctors took the halo off and Barb, my mom and I were on our way out of the hospital. What a day that was.

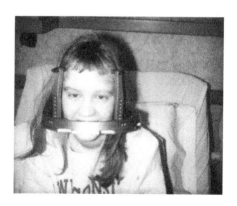

I was happy that was over with and now all we could do was wait for two more months to have another MRI scan and see if the gamma knife procedure helped. So I went on taking that disgusting shark cartilage, carrot juice and all those vitamins. I was visualizing every night and I learned to remove anything negative in my life and stopped hanging around anyone who made me feel even the slightest bit negative. I surrounded myself with positive people, with people that made me feel only happy. I stopped going to events or parties I was going to just to please other people. We all have those kinds of things we think, oh gosh I don't really want to go, but I think I should. Forget it. Not anymore with me. It was all about me now and making my body healthy.

December eventually came which meant it was time for another MRI scan to see if the cancer was gone. We all took the trip back down to the hospital again, all my friends, my mom, and me. My stomach's turning, my hands are shaking, the usual anxiety of a morning of an MRI reading. We finally got the results and the cancer was back again. Oh my, gosh! Are you kidding me?! I had surgery in June, radiation in August, chemotherapy in September, gamma knife in October and its back again! Well what do we have to do next asked my mom, taking the, there's no time for dawdling role, let's move on. Another surgery explains Dr. Vick. But we did that already and it didn't work. This time, we were going to take out the tumor again and place gliadel wafers in my brain. These wafers release chemotherapy right onto the tumor site over a period of six months. "Let's do it." replied my mother, but I wasn't so sure I was ready for another surgery. I was tired of being a patient, so tired of all the procedures. It hadn't even been a whole year and we were going on the third surgery. That is, if you consider gamma knife a surgery and I did since it took just as much out of me, we were in the hospital, there was pain and I was crying. I didn't know if I could do it again. I'll never forget what the surgeon said to me who would be performing the surgery, "This isn't a cure you know, but it will buy you some time." " I know," I replied, but, I didn't know, I didn't know why I was listening to a surgeon telling me I could buy some more time to live a little longer. I didn't know why this was happening to me at the age of twenty-one. I didn't know what I could do to fix it and I didn't know if I wanted to have another surgery. What I did know was that I was exhausted and I hated all of this.

I was supposed to be taking my preschool student teaching course that I already postponed because of the chemotherapy I had taken in the fall semester. And I did know having another surgery meant my mom would have to help me regain my balance, she would need to slowly walk up and down the hospital hallways with me until I was strong enough. She would need to help me wash my hair again and get in and out of the bathtub. I didn't know what to do.

But the thing that changed my mind was the night I was on the phone with my friend Barb and she said to me, "I know you want to give up right now, but you need to push ahead." I think my jaw dropped to the floor when she said it. I couldn't believe that someone actually new and understood how I felt. Just hearing that statement at that moment helped me so much. "You have to take that last bit of energy you have deep inside you and push further one more time." she finished. So I thought a little more about having the surgery and then I received a letter in the mail about my preschool student teaching assignment. I was so nervous because I knew that I might not have been able to handle it, and would the teachers understand that I may be sick a lot or not have much energy because of everything I was going through. I opened the letter and couldn't believe what I read. I was assigned to student teach at the church where I had worked for the last two years. Oh, my, gosh! I couldn't believe it! They knew me there, and they all knew what was going on

49

in my life at the time. I knew I could do it! This was another sign from God. I made my decision to have the surgery.

December 31, 1996 I had another brain surgery. The doctors removed the cancer and placed the gliadel wafers inside my brain. Two months later my friends and I went to The Kellogg Cancer center for another MRI scan. We were waiting in that ever so familiar waiting room. My stomach was turning, I couldn't stop fidgeting with my hands or tapping my feet, or making eye contact with every nurse walking down the hallway waiting for mine. Finally, "Courtney." called the nurse. We went into Dr. Vick's office and he said, "Your scan is good. There's no sign of cancer." What?! Yes!! Hugs! Everyone was hugging, there were smiles, everyone was smiling. Dr. Vick gave me a big hug, it was wonderful. After a year of fighting with every ounce of my body I was finally cancer free!

Life after
Year one

What did I do then? I went on to student teach for the next two semesters and I kept getting an MRI scan every two months eventually changing to every three months. My friends and I went to our first cancer survivor walk and celebration that's held on Chicago's lakefront in June of 1997. I stood up in Barb's wedding in the fall of 1997. Something that doctor up in Mayo clinic told me I wouldn't be here to do. I graduated from college in December of 1997, just a semester behind schedule. I made it! Something else I wasn't supposed to be here to accomplish. That spring I started substitute teaching and eventually got my own job as a kindergarten teacher. I was past cancer and finally moving on with what I always wanted to accomplish.

I became pretty used to getting MRI scans every three months. I always had a friend there with me. Even though we were all in the working world my friends still managed to support me any way they could. Every June we continued to go to the cancer survivor walks and celebration to remember how far we've come. But isn't it just when things are going well, that something pops up to slow you down?

Reoccurrence

It was the spring of 2000, three years later, when I woke up with a horrible feeling in my stomach. I chalked it up to a bad dream, but I should have known then what was going to happen. I had an MRI scan that day and as usual I met a friend at the hospital and we went into Dr. Vick's office together. I was feeling pretty confident because I was getting used to coming in and having clean scans. I'm always nervous of course, but I was used to the cancer free scans. What Dr. Vick said next though were the words no cancer survivor wants to hear. "It looks like the cancer is back. I want to send the scan to another doctor for a second opinion, but it looks to me like its back again."

I wish I could say I was being strong and said, "Okay, what do we do?" But I wasn't. I knew what this meant. My life was going to change horribly. Immediately tears ran down my face, my stomach was sick. I was used to living the cancer free life. This meant more surgery, a shaved head again, weeks of recovery, my mom helping me wash again, having to cut food into little pieces so I could fit them into my mouth. Yes, when they perform brain surgery the muscle above the jaw is cut so the ability to open the mouth real wide is affected so my food had to be cut into small baby pieces so I could place them in my mouth through the small opening. And last, there goes my social life again. And I wonder why I'm still single today! I've spent a big chunk of the last ten years in and out of the hospitals.

And that's what I did. I had surgery again. My life stopped again. It's funny how fast I fell right back into the so called "normal" life of being cancer free. Don't get me wrong though, the thought was always in the back of my head that the cancer might come back as all survivors are familiar with, but I wasn't ready for it. And I sure wasn't ready for what the summer of 2000 had in store for me.

I had surgery right away in June of 2000, but this time I was real nervous for some reason. I don't know why I was more nervous this time than I had been before, maybe because I knew about everything that came along with surgery. I'm not sure why, but I was so nervous that I wrote my own will. I didn't have it notarized or anything official, but I wrote it out, signed and dated it, and told my friends where it was hidden, in my closet underneath my journal, in case anything happened to me during surgery.

As it turned out, there was a reason for my being so nervous. It was a little foreshadowing on what was to come. After that surgery I woke up while the nurse was pulling the tube out of my throat. I starting moaning, because I was too weak to speak or open my eyes and I heard the nurse say, "You won't remember any of this later." Funny thing is that had never happened to me in any other surgery. Then I heard other nurses saying, "She's waking up! What do we do? Can we give her more anesthesia? Ask the doctor!"

That experience was extremely scary for me. Even though I was barely awake, I could still hear the nervous tones in their voices. Thankfully nothing like that happened again.

Well I stayed in the hospital for a week this time and I was ready to go home. Thank goodness. If you have ever stayed in a hospital you know they are no place to rest. Just as you get comfortable and fall asleep after watching all the boring soap operas because you can't find anything else on television a nurse comes in to wake you up and ask you to take some meds. And then the cycle starts all over again, how could I get myself comfortable with all these needles and tubes and only being able to sleep on one side because of the stitches that were on the other side of my head. My mom picked me up and I was thrilled to leave. Wheelchair or not, I was so happy to smell the fresh air.

We left the hospital, my mom driving the car and me in the passenger seat. We stopped at a

Wal-mart so I could use the bathroom. As my mom got out of the car to help me out, I started to get out of the car myself. I thought I was stronger than I really was. As I slowly stood up to get out of the car the door started to close on me and hit my head right on the spot that had just been stitched up from surgery. I fell right back into the passenger seat and dropped my head into my mother's lap. I was crying hysterically because not only was that area sensitive, but I could feel liquid gushing out of my head which was completely freaking me out. "Oh, my, gosh, what did I do? Did I tear the stitches? Did I ruin it? Are we going to need to go back to the hospital?" were the thoughts running through my head. My mom managed to calm me down and the leaking seemed to have stopped after a few minutes so we continued on our drive six hours north. Thinking about it now, the drive must have been extremely hard for my mother trying not to hit any bumps in the road because the slightest movement hurt my head.

We were finally home and my mom helped me into the house where I proceeded to rest on the couch for the next week. But something different was happening that had never happened after surgery before. The right side of my head, the part I had surgery on, was leaking. A clear fluid was slowing dripping down the right side of my head. I was catching it with a small wash cloth which seemed to have worked, but we were concerned so we went to the emergency room anyway to get it checked out. Yippee! I thought, "My favorite place, the hospital." They asked a bunch of questions and determined the stitches looked fine, but to come back in if I got a headache or the chills. We went home relieved, but little did we know what was about to happen.

While sleeping during the middle of the night on July 23, 2000 I woke up a little cold. I was trying to solve the problem and just pulled some more covers onto myself, but I was getting colder and then colder and colder and continued wrapping the covers tighter around myself. Then I needed to go to the bathroom, so I stood up and that's when it hit me like a freight train. I had to close my eyes because my head was pounding, but at the same time it felt like it was spinning around and around in circles like an out of control merry-go-round. As I'm writing this today I still get nauseous thinking about how it felt. So I had to fall back onto the couch. I couldn't stand. I started calling for my mom, but I was so weak and now this pounding and spinning and nausea and now my body was shivering from the cold I felt. It was like I was in the middle of the arctic with no clothes on me.

My parents finally heard my quiet voice and rushed out. My dad called 911 and my mom was throwing blankets upon blankets onto me eventually just lying herself on top of my body to stop my body from shaking. The ambulance finally arrived and my mom asked me if I wanted to walk or wanted a stretcher. Of course I needed the stretcher, she hadn't seen my previous attempt to stand up and use the bathroom. As soon as they put me on the stretcher I started to vomit. I couldn't stop. One after the other, I almost couldn't get a breath in. Finally, when we were in the ambulance I was able to whisper the word Compazine to the EMTs. Compazine was a drug I used to take with chemotherapy so I wouldn't throw up; therefore I knew the drug would have helped me to stop throwing up in the ambulance. Then I heard one EMT ask another, "Can we give her Compazine?" It's extremely disgusting how much more patients know sometimes about health care than the people actually taking care of the patients. They finally gave me some Compazine and I must have fallen asleep after that because I don't remember another thing about that night until I woke up the next morning in the Evanston hospital in Illinois.

The previous night when they realized I had bacterial meningitis we were flown back to the hospital so my surgeon could help me. My mother and I took an emergency flight back to Evanston to speak with the surgeon. Apparently he had another surgery to do at the time we arrived so he spoke with my mother and left. Only a few minutes later he came back and told my mom he had given it some thought and decided that I needed to be operated on immediately. Of course I am very grateful for that today.

I woke up the next morning with my mom sitting next to me. "What happened?" I asked and she explained everything to me. In came a doctor and I introduced myself as he proceeded to remind me that we met the night before, none of which I remembered. He then explained that because of the meningitis my entire bone flap, in people terms, skull in the area that was operated on, was infected and had to be removed along with all of the chemotherapy wafers that were just put into my brain to keep the cancer away.

Let me summarize that. I had surgery to remove the cancer and the Gliadel wafers were put in to release chemotherapy into my brain and fight the remaining microscopic cancer. I got bacterial meningitis, the wafers were taken out and my bone flap, part of my skull was removed. But the problems just kept on flowing. I needed what is called a lumbar drain now put into my back to drain the spinal fluid. I was brought into a hospital room on a stretcher and had one nurse standing in front of me with two doctors seated behind me. They wouldn't allow me to take any drugs to relieve the pain for this procedure because the doctors needed me to tell them which leg I felt the pain in that they were about to put me through. That is correct. You did just read that correctly. I had to let the doctors know what leg the excruciating pain they were going to inflict on me was affecting. Once again I found myself in another procedure where I couldn't be given any pain relievers. I was starting to become familiar with how the people must have lived way back when there were no medications for pain. And oh, my, gosh! You couldn't have prepared me for the amount of pain I was about to feel.

What they did was slowly push a tube into my back. "Ahhhh!" I screamed. "What leg?" the doctors asked. I yelled "the left leg, the left!" and so on as the procedure continued switching from the left to the right as the tube changed its path. "The right leg! The right!" In the middle of my screams I was trying to calm myself down realizing no one was going to help me, I had to help myself so I tried to do some heavy deep breathing and talk myself into it not being so bad, but then another shot of pain would go down a leg and I would yell, "Left leg! Left leg!" Still today, I cringe when I think back to the experience. I just couldn't believe in today's day and age that patients could still be put through that kind of pain. I wouldn't wish it on my worst enemy. Well, maybe my worst.

I had this tube in my back for a total of two long weeks. You may be wondering how someone functions with a tube in their back. What I had to do was lye on my left side in the hospital bed the entire time. I had a catheter to use the bathroom.

Not a very pleasant experience, but all a part of illness as many of us survivors understand, if it's not one medical procedure, it's another. So I just had to maintain some small amount of comfort to watch television and sleep.

It was finally time to get the tube out of my back, Praise Jesus! I was very excited, but of course it wasn't without worry. Now we had to see if my own ventricle tube in my body was working to drain the spinal fluid on it's own after the meningitis. How did we figure that out? We had to watch my head after the lumbar drain was taken out of my back. If the right side of my head stayed flat like normal that meant my ventricle tube was still working, but if it started getting puffy that meant it wasn't working.

The doctor took the tube out right there in my room and the nurse helped me stand up. We looked into the mirror and what do you know? My head was getting puffy! My own ventricle tube wasn't working anymore! What did this mean? Another surgery! This would have been my third surgery in two months! I was going back under because they needed to put a shunt in me to work as my own ventricle tube. "Oh, my, gosh! Somebody slap me! Another f*@king surgery!!! Am I in hell?"

I needed to go back into surgery, but this time my mom couldn't be there. She had taken too much time off work as it was; there was no way she could make it. Going into surgery is scary in itself, let alone not having anyone with you when you wake up. Maybe I'm spoiled. So what happened? My wonderful, wonderful friends stepped up to the plate again. Kris, one of my roommates from college said she would be there for the surgery. Once again I need to reiterate the large support group I had to help me through this cancer ordeal.

I went back into surgery and they placed a shunt into my body. It's about the size of a spaghetti noodle. It went into the top of my head and runs down the left side of my head continuing down my neck, across my chest and ends at the bottom of the left side of my stomach. I can actually follow it almost all the way down with my hands, losing it a little bit around my chest area, but then picking it up again around my stomach. This time the doctors had to make a two to three inch incision in the bottom of my stomach which is where the shunt drains.

Let us remember that brain surgery is not very painful. It's very uncomfortable and takes a bit to recover from it all, but for the majority not very painful. But this time the doctors cut into my stomach area. That was a whole different story. Anyone who has had surgery can relate I'm sure. It was very painful. I remember being rolled into my hospital room. I couldn't open my eyes because I was very weak from surgery, I couldn't say anything, but I knew I was feeling a lot of pain.

It was then that I felt someone grab my hand. It was Kris! She was there just like she said she would be! I was so happy! I can't explain even today how good holding her hand made me feel. I couldn't see her because I couldn't open my eyes, and I couldn't talk with her, but I knew she was there. That thought alone, was all the comfort I needed. When I couldn't have my mom, I could have my friend. Of course still today I don't believe that I have thanked her enough for being there that day. I don't think that I ever can because I will never be able to convey to her the kind of warmth and comfort she was able to give me on that day in the hospital.

The recovery Again

I eventually left the hospital after spending almost half of the summer there. I refer to that summer as the summer I spent in hell. It wasn't a good time at all, but I had to keep on. Now, after all that we weren't sure what was going to happen because remember, after all the meningitis and other complications the chemotherapy wafers were taken out of my head because they were infected. That was what we were using to fight the cancer and now they were gone. What were we supposed to do now was the question.

Dr. Vick already had a plan. There was a new chemotherapy Drug for brain cancer. A brand new drug; as a matter of fact! At that time it was the first new drug for brain cancer in twenty years. This chemotherapy wasn't available when I was first diagnosed in 1996. So it seemed after all, all of this fighting and "buying some time" was worth it. There was something new available to help. The only scary part was it seemed to work on some people and not on others. Why? The doctors didn't know.

Before I started on this new chemo I had to recover a bit from all the surgeries that I went through over the summer. So I would lie around on the couch resting the majority of the day with a short walk to the bathroom here and there. I had all of these wonderful cheery balloons to look at all day long that eventually seemed to be just starring at me, almost mocking me. Remember I had been lying there for so long, on and off, back home and then back to the hospital. Not feeling like myself, no energy for what seemed to be such a long time. Those smiley faced balloons started to piss me off. I remember one day I just couldn't stand looking at that yellow, happy smiling face anymore. My brother was in the kitchen and I asked him to get me a steak knife. He did, although he must have thought my request was a little strange. I slowly stood up, walked over to that enormous, yellow, smiley faced balloon and proceeded to stab it as I yelled, "Die! You bastard, Die! And what a relief it was to not have that happy little f*@king face staring at me anymore.

Although that slight breakdown might make me seem a bit off balance it was a very positive step forward in my healing process. Remember, getting out all of those negative feelings helps in the healing process.

Along with stabbing balloons, I was also taking injections on a daily basis to cure the meningitis. At first I had a nurse who would come to my parents' home everyday to inject me with the medication. I had an indwelling port which is a small round thing placed under the skin in my arm to use to stick the needles into instead of my veins so they didn't collapse. A home health nurse, what a wonderful thing you would think. However, a good majority of the time she couldn't get the needle into the port, so she would stick me with a needle, move the needle around to try and make it work, then take the needle out and stick me again. Our dog Rascal would sit right next to me whining while tears would be streaming down my face because of those painful sticks over and over again into my arm. Come to find out she was using the wrong size needle! It was too big!

Well eventually I was left to do the injections on my own. At that point my arm was accessed which meant I had a needle in my arm connected to some tubing at all times so I could continue taking the injections without the nurse. I wouldn't have to stick myself with the needle, all I had to do was stick the needle into the tubing that was connected to the needle already sticking into my arm. Sounds a little tricky, but it was fairly easy. And oh my, gosh, talk about feeling stress. I remember the day the home health nurse showed me how to do this whole procedure. I started crying because I was so scared to get it wrong.

I had to make sure I clamped the tubes before sticking the needle with the medication in so no air bubbles would get into the tubes that were connected to my veins. So I had to clamp one tube, while unclamping another and inject into the unclamped tube and Oh, my, gosh! If there were air bubbles that slipped through, the machine holding the bag of medication would start beeping, BEEP! BEEP! BEEP! Yes, did I mention while I took the injections I was connected to a machine that was holding the bag of medication. The machine would beep to let me know there were air bubbles in the tube and I would have to clamp and unclamp the tubing, flick the tubing to try and get the air bubbles out, because if the air got into my veins it would be really, really bad, and then I would start the process all over again. Wow, does that explanation make you feel like taking a nap?

Well, I did it! I figured out the machine. I mastered the clamping and unclamping and the flicking of the air bubbles, wrapping Saran Wrap around my arm and sticking it in a Ziploc bag everytime I showered, and whew! Another battle tackled on this marathon called cancer.

Alternative therapies

But of course we weren't leaving everything up to the doctor's treatments alone. The statistics on that spoke very clearly, I was going to die. All these treatments and new chemotherapies were just buying me some time. And because of that we were also very much into any alternative therapies we could find. Over the course of the last few years while I was still cancer free I had been reading any books that I could find about people being healed and miracles being performed. One of the books I happen to read was called, Blessed by Miracles, by William Burt that gave several examples of places to visit and people who healed others. I highlighted all the places and people that were fairly close to us just in case the cancer came back. Well, it was a good thing I kept up on my research because one of the names I found was of a priest who performed hands-on healing to others, Father Peter Rookey. The amazing part about him was that he performed miracles right there in Chicago! It was perfect! I couldn't find anyone closer than him.

I had been to a "hands-on" healing service once before and obviously it didn't work, but this man had so many different experiences healing people. These people came from all over the world to see him and he was so close to me. We had to see him. I understand that most people think believing in things like this is ridiculous, but how quickly your thinking changes when you start living on hope. We were ready to try anything, which in the end, I believe was the key to surviving.

My mother called around and found the old, catholic church he was working in and we went to one of his services. We were amazed to see that there were bus loads of people at this church to see this priest. The first thought on most people's minds is, he was there for the money. But there was no charge to see Father Rookey. My mom and I slowly walked into the church, my mom looking like a normal person, me with my bandana on to hide the bald circles on both sides of my head and the needle and tubing hanging from my left arm. You could definitely tell by looking at us who the sick person was who needed to be healed.

This church was so old, it was historic, a beautiful church. The architecture was a kind like we never see anymore. The pews were filled with people from all over the world, everyone there with the hope to be healed of their illness. The only place left to sit was so far back from the front we didn't think the priest would ever get to us. But after we sat down I noticed a few pews in the front that were roped off and labeled, terminally ill. Hallelujah! That was me! As much as I didn't like to refer to myself as terminally ill, the fact of the matter was that was the category I fell into. So with my bandana on my head and a needle hanging out of my arm, I stood up and said "Mom, we're moving up to the front." And that's exactly what we did. I was now feeling very confident that Father Rookey would get to us during the service.

While we were sitting up front watching the hundreds of people file into the church a woman approached me and handed me a small medal with the picture of Mary on it. I now know it to be called, the miraculous medal created in 1830. The woman said to me, "Here, this was blessed by the Medjugorie in Yugoslavia. You need it more than I do, keep it." Oh, my, gosh! I couldn't believe she had given me that healing medal, and it was blessed by the Medjugorie! That is a well known place where many people have been miraculously healed, a place that I could never get to, because it was too far away. I was so grateful and still am today.

The service eventually started and we saw Father Rookey. He looked very weak, and shaky. I was concerned with how such a feeble looking man could help us. He started talking and his voice seemed much stronger than he looked. We did many Hail Mary's which was different for my mom and I because we're Methodist, so we did the best we could to follow along. Father Rookey started calling people up to the front of the church one pew at a time. People would walk up and stand in a row side by side facing him while he walked from one person to the next touching them and praying. I remember hearing people clapping because of the miracles that were going on around us. I remember looking around and thinking I couldn't believe I was there at something like that with so many sick people around us. You'd think I would have been used to it by then, but I never did get used to what I was living. It was always like I was in a dream or a movie.

I saw a woman come into the church in a wheelchair, and watched her walk out with a cane. But was it real, or just for show, to make people believers? Regardless, I had to believe. If I wanted to survive there was no room for doubt in my mind. If I wanted to survive I had to believe that God was going to heal me through this priest. We also met a couple who was there to heal their son. They had come once before and it hadn't worked, but they were going to try until it did work. I had to reassure myself it was going to work for me because any ounce of doubt would mean that I didn't truly believe and therefore I would not be healed.

It was finally our turn to go up to the front of the church. We all formed a row in front of the priest, all of us facing him. My mom stood right behind me, while he moved from one person to the next. He would hold his hand on the person at the same time saying a prayer and then move on to the next. When he came to me he touched my head and prayed silently as I prayed also. For some reason he kept his hand on me a lot longer than he had the others in my row. I'm not sure what that meant, or why he did, so I continued to pray with my eyes closed and head down until I heard my mom say, "Honey, we're done." We walked down from the middle step and my mom said, 'Did you notice he kept his hand on you longer than the others?" And I had noticed! It wasn't just what I thought, but my mom noticed too. Why did he do that? I have always assumed it was because he could feel the intensity of my illness just months to live.

That was a very positive experience for me. I still have his card with his picture and name on it, along with the miraculous medal that the woman gave me. I often rub it against my head just in case I need a little extra healing.

Chemo Again

Even though I had that incredible healing experience and was taking the injections for the meningitis, I still had to start taking that new chemotherapy, Temodar. I was nervous, but at the same time I was optimistic that maybe this chemotherapy was the cure for me. Even though every time I asked Dr. Vick millions of questions about the chemo he could never give me the answer I was looking for, that Temodar was going to cure me. Every time I saw him, I kept on asking, "Could it be a cure? Has it cured some people? What are people doing that it doesn't cure?" And on and on. That must have been so annoying for him, but the only answers he could give me were, "We don't know. We do know it helps some people, and not others." but why? They didn't know, but I wanted to know. They of course couldn't give me that answer. As much as they would have liked to have those answers, the drug was too new. What they could tell me was "sometimes it worked, and sometimes it didn't."

"Are there any side effects?" I asked. It wasn't like I had a choice not to take the drug if there were side effects. This was my only hope to live any longer. I had no choice but to take the Temodar, I was just curious about the side effects. One side effect they new of, once again at that time the drug was so new they didn't know much about side effects yet, was that I could get Leukemia. What! So let me get this straight. These were my two choices: do nothing and die in a few months, or take the chemotherapy and risk getting Leukemia later and die then. I chose the latter. They weren't telling me that not everyone got Leukemia who took this drug, it was a maybe. So of course, I started the Temodar.

The first night I started the Temodar I was at my cousin Heather's house. She's a nurse, a perfect place for me to be. I was sitting in a chair in the living room and she was across the room from me on the floor. This was a very, very, very, big moment for me because the Temodar came in huge pills that I had to swallow. And remember, up until this point in my life I had never swallowed big pills, or little pills for that matter. I had to crush them with my pill crusher, mix them in with some applesauce and swallow them like that. All of my antibiotics that I had ever taken throughout my 21 years of life had been liquids. Big pills meant big problems. I couldn't take the Temodar capsules apart, I couldn't crush the pill with my pill crusher and I couldn't even try to hide it in some food. I even had to fast for two hours before and two hours after I took the pill. And I could only swallow them with water, a lot of water. I had no idea how I was going to do this. And to freak me out even more, the warning labels on the Temodar read, Do not open capsule, do not let powder touch your skin and do not breathe in powder-Toxic. Oh my, gosh! Toxic! It's Toxic!? Why are they giving me toxic stuff to put in my body? That was like sweat dripping down my face anxiety and fear to figure out how I was going to swallow the thing and then hope I didn't gag on the capsule, have it open up in my throat and then the powder would be touching me, and what would happen then? There would be toxic powder touching me! Who do you call when there's toxic stuff touching you? So you can sense the amount of fear I was feeling at that point. For most people that would have been a piece of cake, and that's great for them, but for me, I was about to take a step into hell, again.

My cousin Heather was sitting across from me because of all this anxiety I was having. My wonderful, calm cousin explains to me that maybe by the time the pills are in my stomach and digested with all the water I needed to drink to take them that may not be toxic anymore. Her logic made sense to me and helped me get over my little freak out session. And now it was time to swallow the pill. To take off some pressure Heather said, "Okay, I won't look at you." Isn't that what we all say when we want someone to do something really bad. It works. I put the water in my mouth, and then put the pill in my mouth, and after a few swishes around my mouth I swallowed the pill! We were both so excited! Amen! On to the next battle, how was it going to make me feel? Not knowing the answer to that question, I quickly went to bed.

The next morning I woke up not feeling the best. I thought I had to go to the bathroom, but when I was on the toilet I thought I was going to throw up, so I yelled to Heather for a basket to throw up into. She ran in with a bucket, but nothing happened and I knew I wasn't going to use the bathroom, so I jumped onto the floor and just rested my head on the toilet to throw up but just a little came out. A few minutes later I got up and ate a bowl of peanut butter captain crunch cereal and I felt so much better. And another step conquered. Yes!

Now from being in and out of the hospital for so long my body still wasn't functioning correctly.

What I mean by that is I was extremely constipated, and to make matters worse I was taking
Zofran with the chemotherapy which was supposed to keep me from throwing up, but one of
the side effects of the Zofran was constipation. At
that point I was thinking, come on, can you give
a girl a break? I had never nor have I ever experienced such horrible pain from being constipated.
The sharp, knife stabbing pain went all the way
up the left side of my body into my neck. I could
only move certain ways in order for me not to feel
the pain. And of course the doctors, prescribed
me Senokot to help with the problem, but all that
did was to send me running to the bathroom with
horrible, gut wrenching cramping and no results.
Not like cancer itself isn't enough to deal with,
but it's all the side effects that come along with it
that makes the fight so hard.

Moving on with life

Shortly after I started the Temodar it was time for me to start teaching again. And of course I wanted to continue teaching. There was no question in my mind. I needed any amount of normalcy that I could get in my life, but my head was still half shaved from the surgeries and only half of my bangs were shaved off also along with a skull sized upside down horseshoe shaped scar on the right side of my head. I couldn't go into work looking like that. I taught kindergarten. The kids would have run away screaming in fear of the monster that was their teacher. So I asked my principal if I could wear a bandana to school and she sounded a little hesitant as I could understand it wasn't the typical dress code, but she agreed. And that's what I did. Someone braided the back of my hair and I folded a bandana kind of into a blindfold width and wrapped it around my head so it covered my forehead and most of the incision. It wasn't your typical bandana wearing cancer look so I felt pretty confident in going back to work. I was so happy to be on my way back. I went with the bandana on my head, the needle and tubing hanging out of my arm and the incredible amount of pain I was still having from the constipation that wouldn't quit. I didn't care, I was so happy to be alive and strong enough to work.

I still had to give myself those hour long injections every morning to fight the meningitis. And because the injections were so long, some days I just didn't have time before work to get them done, so I had to do them while I was teaching. I would do it during our calendar time in the classroom first thing in the morning. The children would be sitting on the carpet in front of me and I would be sitting on my chair connected to the machine that was holding the bag of medication. Of course during the course of our calendar time the machine would start beeping because of those air bubbles I talked about earlier and I would have to stop and do the clamping, the unclamping, the flicking of the tube, the re-clamping, and we would continue on with calendar time. My kindergarten students were very curious about what everything was, the needles, the machine and the bag of liquid. What was it all for, why did I have to do that. I gave them a simple explanation that just like some of them took medication when they were sick, I had to take medication too, but mine was through a tube. They completely understood. Explain it in simple terms, and children understand everything.

I continued teaching that semester while taking those injections and still taking that new chemotherapy drug. Those constipation pains of course were just getting worse because I was taking more and more chemo and more Zofran and getting more and more constipated, and they hurt so badly. One day while I was teaching I had so much pain going up the entire left side of my body that I could not even stand up straight. So to deal with this and still go to work I told my students we were going to have sideways day, because when I stood with my body tilted sideways I couldn't feel the pain. Again, I was teaching kindergarten, so they loved the idea. I got to teach, they got to learn, and I didn't hurt. It was a successful day all around.

Let me tell you after so many days of feeling like I did, my optimism was starting to fade. It seemed to be getting too hard to continue living a life with this problem. I was in pain all of the time. And to top it off, my nurse told me my blood work was so good they wanted to increase the amount of chemotherapy I was taking from one pill a day to three pills a day. On one hand I guess that had was good news to know my body was tolerating the drug, but on the other hand it meant no relief for my body and how I was feeling.

One of the reasons I was able to fight so hard was because I knew God was with me. I knew He was walking by my side, but at this point I was getting real tired of the way I was feeling. Let me reiterate very tired, I didn't know if I could keep doing this and I really just started. So on the way home that day I was driving in the middle lane on the Interstate. I was talking with God and said "Father, if this is how the rest of my life is going to be, I don't want to be here anymore." I was exhausted. At the exact second I finished that statement a car crept up real slowly on my left side. It was weird because the left lane is for passing and cars usually cruise by on that side. But this car was just kind of hanging around, slowly going by. So I looked over and the license plate read nvrgvup. Oh, my, gosh! Never give up! God already gave me an answer. I was surrounded by angels! I couldn't give up, I had to push through the suffering and trust God that I will be okay. And once again, my spirits were lifted and I was given a little more strength to move on.

I continued to teach all the while taking the Temodar five days a month. So I would take 3 pills five days in a row while taking the chemo. I couldn't eat or drink while taking the pills and would have to drink tons of water with the Temo-dar so water is something I still can't drink alone. It makes me nauseous. I was extremely nauseous during those weeks and very tired, but I had no choice to stop. I would try all different kinds of food to settle my stomach. What did the trick was saltine crackers and 7-up. And of course there's always gotta be some other type of obstacle to deal with. During that fall I had some ignorant teacher's aide in my room who took pleasure in telling my principal I wasn't well enough to teach. In her words, "I was just falling apart in there." She complained so much that a district adminis-trator was brought in to observe me. And her con-clusion was, "I think she's fantastic." Ha! I really can't stand people who have nothing better to do than complain about others. Especially when the others are fighting cancer.

But being in the position I was in health wise, I had no time to waste my thoughts and energy on those things. I had to focus on stay-ing healthy. That meant I needed to take the

Temodar every month, drink the carrot juice everyday, surround myself with laughter and only people with positive thoughts and energy and lastly continue to visualize at night before falling asleep in bed. Even if it was just for five minutes a night I needed to keep visualizing my brain free of cancer. Sometimes I would bulldoze the cancer off of my brain, others I would use Pacman to eat all of the cancer cells. But what seemed to work the best was using a small pointed magnet like a pen to clean up all the cancer cells and then I would dip the pen into a bowl of water. Sort of like putting out a cigarette in a bowl of water. In my mind it made that singe sound and the cancer cells were gone just like the ashes of a cigarette in water would sound. Then I could put the magnet back on my brain to collect more of the bad cells off of my brain. All of that kind of sounds like there was a lot involved, but it worked the best and the fastest for me.

I know some people reading this are thinking it's just crazy to believe in those kinds of things, but mind over matter truly works. Just like the positive thinking works. I had a mind over matter experience as a child that backs that that theory up. At a birthday party in the seventh grade we decided to play the game, light as a feather, stiff as a board. What we did was have one girl lying on the floor and the rest of us sat around her body on our knees with our heads down and eyes closed. Each of us, maybe four or five put two fingers under the body lying on the floor. Then we would chant, she's sick, she's sick, she's sick, she's dying, she's dying, she's dying, she's dead, she's dead, she's dead. Then the leader would say, let's lift her body and with only two of our fingers, eight in total we would lift the person all the way up until we were all standing and she was lying on our fingers as high as our wastes. We were in complete shock, but did this over and over again. When we broke our concentration the person would fall to the ground and we would laugh in disbelief. That is a perfect example of the power of thought. If I believe something to be true and meditate and pray on that thought I can make it happen.

I still visualize at night after I say my prayers I visualize my brain to be cancer free before I fall asleep.

Celebration

In May 10, 2006, now on the Temodar for six years I went into my Doctor's office for my usual MRI scan, except this one was different. I was a little more nervous than normal and had two friends come with me this time. If this scan was okay it would mean I had survived for ten years. Ten years! Remember the doctor in the hospital told me I would die within the year, but a nurse also said one person had survived ten years and that it was possible. And here we were ten years later. My stomach was turned upside down. The nurse called us in, Dr. Vick looked at me, I handed him the scans, and we all sat down. I sat directly across from Dr. Vick like I always did and Kris and Bev sat to the right side of me. We all watched Dr. Vick as he held up the scans to compare them to the last scans. My stomach was still turning, my hands couldn't stop shaking, and he finally spoke.

It looks good. Except this time instead of asking, "Are you sure?" like I always did I started crying. I was so happy and excited I had made it this far that I started crying. I didn't like to cry in front of Dr. Vick because I didn't want to show him any weakness so I quickly apologized and explained that I was just so happy. Kris and Bev then explained that it's been ten years, and we were so excited because it was the ten year mark. He replied with, "Ten years doesn't mean anything though. It isn't a significant number." And that's of course the doctor talking. To him ten years wasn't a significant number when dealing with this type of brain cancer. It didn't mean I was in remission, it didn't mean I could stop chemo and it didn't mean the cancer wouldn't come back. But what it did mean was that I was still living ten years after being diagnosed with an astrocytoma glioblastoma grade four tumor. It meant that I was in the top two percent in the world at that point surviving that long. And that I did what the nurse in the hospital said was possible, but not common. I fought, and I fought, and I fought hard and I was still here ten years later. Amen!

Continuing on

I continued on with the Temodar for many years to follow and went on teaching. Of course brain cancer couldn't be the only bump in the road. I went on to find out I had a funny mole that turned out to be melanoma, removed from my knee. The doctor said we removed it all, don't worry about it stay out of the sun always. After that I had a few more removed that turned out to have bad cells also, so again stay out of the sun and we keep checking every six months. But after a few more years on the Temodar I started to become allergic to many different things. First it was kiwi fruit which I loved. My lips became real puffy when I ate the fruit. Next it was lip liner. My lips filled with all of these little bumps and got real itchy when I used the liner. After that I became allergic to my deodorant. I couldn't stop itching under my left armpit eventually spreading to my right. Then my eyes were itching so badly I had to stop using my eye liner. For a person who has never had an allergic reaction to anything in her life, this was quite odd.

We were assuming these were all the side effects from the Temodar I was having. Then my tongue had turned green. I mean there was this green coating on my tongue that I couldn't scrape off to save my life and finally, I was forgetting my words. When I would talk I would have to describe things in order to get the words out because I couldn't think of the words. For example, I couldn't think of the word slipper so I would say, you know those things you put on your feet to stay warm. And this made it extremely difficult to teach. I would explain something to my class and have to say, that thing over there.

It was at that point we decided it was time to cut back on the chemotherapy. When I say we I mean my doctor, my nurse and I decided this was probably a good choice. See there was one other patient that had been on the Temodar as well, but he wasn't having any of these side effects. We had to cut back on the Temodar, there was no other choice. This was a very scary thought for me. Just writing it down on paper makes my stomach turn. I was alive at that point because of that medication, cutting back seemed very risky. I was originally taking five days a week per month, but I was starting to become more and more nauseous every month and it was harder and harder for me to take the full five days of pills. So I secretly cut my own dose down to four days a week. I had done that for the last four months and still had a good scan so we knew four days a month worked. We decided to cut back to three days a month.

Dr. Vick couldn't tell me if it would still by okay of course. This was all trial and error. He didn't know what would happen anymore than anyone else. I didn't know what to do. In one aspect the thought of cutting back on the chemotherapy was so incredibly exciting. I thought I had to be sick for a week every month for the rest of my life. And now I had the choice of cutting back. This was also very scary, what if the cancer came back? I couldn't handle anymore. But oh, my, gosh! What if it still works at just three days a week? How wonderful! So I did it. Cut back to taking the Temodar just three days a month.

By the time I went back to work in August my body was feeling so good. It was absolutely amazing the way I was feeling. For the last ten years I had been either throwing up, in surgery, or lying around to recover. And for the last five years I had been sick for one week every month. It sucked! And I wonder why I'm single today.

But now my body was starting to heal. Even though I was still taking chemotherapy, I wasn't taking it long enough to feel very nauseous anymore. The first and second days were usually okay. I was starting to feel great. My parents told me I was looking better, when I started school that year I actually had enough energy to help out teaching after school and not drop to the couch for an hour after work. Now we had to pray that this dose was still working and keeping the brain cancer away.

All happiness aside, I still worried whether it was working or not, but my body was feeling so good and healthy I couldn't believe that the Temodar wasn't working. Our bodies tell us when something is wrong with our health. We know when we feel a pain that's not supposed to be there that something's wrong. This is the same way we know if our bodies our healthy, we feel good.

In the fall of 2006 I found out I had a nodule on my thyroid, so of course fighting cancer so long already my mind went to, "What are ya kiddin' me??" Thyroid cancer!! After all this bullshit I need more? The doctor reassured me if it was Thyroid cancer it's easy to fight and not to worry at all. Easy for that fool to say, he hadn't been fightin' this crap for ten years already. So to make a long story short I had a few appointments with him and the nodule shrunk at some point leaving the doctor to say it's probably nothing and I haven't gone back since. If it's gonna get me, it can get me. I was done.

Shortly after that I had secretly cut back on chemotherapy to only two days a week and eventually down to just one day a week. I think Dr. Vick really wanted me to stop by that point altogether because he kept reiterating that nobody knew the side effects of someone being on the Temodar as long as I had. But he couldn't actually tell me to stop because he didn't know what would happen either. Would the cancer come back? If so I could always go back on the Temodar and maybe it would shrink the tumor, but we didn't know. Then again, he also said that me taking just the one pill of the Temodar was probably not doing much. He said it was like taking a half of a Tylenol for a headache.

I debated back and forth for a long time, but I was scared. I didn't want to stop the Temodar and have the cancer return. I was beating the odds at that point. It was a miracle, a true miracle. I was still alive. Should I mess with that? I didn't know. I just kept taking one pill for five days a month. It was November of 2008, I had my routine MRI scan and everything was still good. We had our usual discussion. Should I stay on the Temodar or should I stop? I left with the thought that I would continue on the Temodar. Then read the letter that Dr. Vick writes after he sees me and sends out to all the other doctor's that were involved with my case to keep them updated. He had written that all was good and that he shared with me all he knew about the side effects and yet I still wanted to keep taking the Temodar and that he supported my decision. After reading his letter I felt like he really did want me to stop the chemotherapy, but just couldn't tell me because he didn't know for sure what would happen. It wasn't only that, that changed my mind though. I had been praying and praying on this to God. What should I do? What should I do Father? And then one afternoon while visiting my parents' house I will never forget the moment. I was standing in their living room and I got this strong sharp feeling in my body. It wasn't a voice, but it was a feeling that I was done with cancer. It's okay to stop the treatments because I was done. I had a similar feeling when I was first diagnosed with cancer. I was lying on my couch in college while my girlfriend was sitting on the end complaining about a problem with a guy she was dating. I thought to myself, 'I wish I could be worrying about that instead of whether I will live or die.' At that moment I got this sharp, strong feeling that said, 'you will.' Again, it wasn't a voice, it was an incredibly strong feeling that I can only explain as that.

So the point of this is that the feeling I had back then was right, and this feeling was just as incredibly strong I knew it was right too. After talking this over with my friends I decided to stop the chemotherapy altogether. I talked it over with my friends and not my family because I didn't want them to worry. My friend Kim suggested after I stopped the Temodar that I should have an MRI scan in two months rather than waiting four. And that's what I did. My friend Kris met me at Dr. Vick's office on Wednesday, January 23, 2008 at 9:30.

Of course I was even more nervous than usual having stopped the Temodar completely. Dr. Vick came out to get me, which was odd because in 11 and a half years he had never once come to the waiting room to get me. My nurse Annette always came out. Oh, my, gosh! That made me even more nervous thinking something must have been wrong. Why in the world did he come and get me? He asked me, "Why are you back so soon?" Remember I went back in only two months instead of waiting four months. That's when I told him I stopped taking the Temodar and my friends thought I should come back sooner. We kind of smiled at each other because I always made those big decisions without consulting him first.

We walked into his office and there was a social worker sitting in there also. Oh, my, gosh! I thought, Dr. Vick came out to get me and there's a social worker in the Office! The cancer must be back! I was sure of it. There had never been a social worker in the office before. There were often medical students, but never social workers. I thought for sure she was there to console me when he gave me the bad news. Here we are again, I need your strength Father is what I was saying in my head. But then he read the scan. It looks good. Yes! We were so happy! Smiles all over the room, hugs again. Relief. I stopped taking chemotherapy and the cancer did not come back. It's a breakthrough! Does that mean after so many months or years of treatments a person can be cured? Who Knows? No one really. It had only been two months without the Temodar, but almost a year of just taking one pill for five days in a row, so that was kind of like I wasn't taking anything either. Eleven and a half years later and my fight seemed to be over. We couldn't believe it. A goal that I thought was unattainable.

It is now January of 2014, I am still living without any chemotherapy treatments. The cancer has not come back since taking the Temodar for eight years and being healed by Father Rookey. I just celebrated my seventeenth year surviving when my friends and family joined me at the Cancer Survivor's Walk and Celebration on Chicago's lakefront in June of last year. Something we had started after my first year of fighting in 1997. Something that radiologist at the Mayo Clinic said would never happen, 100% guarantee.

What I have learned is that nothing is 100%. And that everything does not happen for a reason. I used to believe that everything did happen for a reason, but it's not true. Things just happen. Good things and bad things happen to all people for no apparent reasons at all. It's been fifteen years, and I have yet to figure out a reason why this happened. But I can rest in the thought that

I am cancer free for good. It's over and I know it's over for good because of that feeling God gave me when I decided to stop the Temodar. I still see Dr. Vick for my MRI scans every 5 months, and after looking at my scans which are now on a compact disc instead of films, I always hear him say under his breath…"unbelievable."

Made in the USA
Monee, IL
18 December 2022

22699627R00066